My First Holiday Cookbook

My First Holiday Cookbook

Written by Valerie Doty
Illustrated by Kathy Jones

First Edition
Edited by Valerie Doty and Richard Goulde
Illustrated by Kathy Jones
English
Bound and Published by Lulu.com
United States of America

Copyright © 2018 by Valerie Doty and Kathy Jones

All rights reserved. This book or any portion thereof may not be reproduced or used in any manner whatsoever without the express written permission of the editor or illustrator.

This is a work of fiction. Names, characters, businesses, places, events and incidents are either the products of the author's imagination or used in a fictitious manner. Any resemblance to actual persons, living or dead, or actual events is purely coincidental.

ISBN 978-1-7336252-0-3

In Memory of Madeline Jones

Table of Contents:

The Gift...5
New Year's Day...6
      Easy Cornbread Casserole...8
      Good Luck Black-Eyed Peas...9
      Black Forest Gooey Goodness...10
Valentine's Day...12
      Creamy Beef Stroganoff...14
      Dreamy Horseradish Salad...15
      Chocolate Chip Bundt Cake...16
Happy Easter...18
      Dijon Vinaigrette Salad...20
      Aaaaw Gratin Potatoes...21
      Crusty Cobbler...22
Mother's Day Breakfast in Bed...24
      Ham n' Cheese Breakfast Casserole...26
      Black Cherry Salad...27
      Caramel Monkey Bread...28
Father's Day...30
      Pulled Pork...32
      Potatoes Parmesan...33
      Cole Slaw...33
      Banana Pudding Cake...34
Fourth of July Picnic...36
      Independence Day Strawberry Cake...38
      Berries n' Cream Finger Jell-O...39
Halloween...42
      Pretzel Bites...44
      Peanut Butter Tarts...45
      Candy Bar Brownies...46
Thanksgiving Day...48
      Turkey and Stuffing...50
      Cranberry Fluff...51
      Sweet Potato Casserole...52
      Haystacks...53
      Pumpkin Pie Cake...54
Merry Christmas ...56
      Lasagna...58
      Garlic Sticks...59
      Mini-Cheesecakes...60
      Seven Layer Salad...61

The Gift

By 5 a.m. on Christmas morning, Grandma was already sitting by the Christmas tree, rocking slowly. She wanted to see the look of joy and wonder on her granddaughter's face as soon as Maddie came running from her bedroom.

She was not disappointed. Maddie burst into the room suddenly, and the house exploded with her joyous cries of "Santa came! Santa came!"

Wrapping paper flew as the gifts were ripped open, one after another: a new doll Maddie had wanted, along with lots of doll clothes, new electronic games, and a giant box from Grandma (who was known for disguising her gifts by wrapping them in odd-sized boxes). Maddie dove into the big box, tossing out handful after handful of packing paper, until she finally emerged with a book and two matching aprons.

"A book???" she thought. Books were fun to read, sure, but Christmas was a time for toys and games, not books! Maddie was already reading in school, at the library, in church, and before bed, so today was supposed to be about playing with toys.

Even though Maddie didn't see the book as the perfect gift, she still ran over and gave Grandma a big hug. Grandma picked up Maddie's new book and read the title out loud: **My First Holiday Cookbook**.

"I will come over every holiday next year," she promised the young girl, "and we will cook together. Won't that be fun?"

Maddie nodded and smiled. She knew whenever Grandma came over, they would have a wonderful day together, but she didn't yet realize how much that little cookbook would mean to her by the end of the next year. Her least favorite present today would soon become her most treasured gift ever.

Grandma came over to babysit on New Year's Eve. Mom and Dad were going to a big party and wouldn't be home until late, so Grandma was going to stay the night.

After dinner, Grandma said, "Maddie, go get the book I gave you for Christmas, and let's get ready for tomorrow." She went on to explain the importance of reading recipes ahead of time: "Not only do we need to make sure we have all the ingredients before we start, we also need to know if there are tasks to start early or the night before."

Then they read through the recipes for New Year's Day to make sure they had all the ingredients. They didn't, but a quick trip to the store solved that problem. Once they had unpacked their groceries, Grandma suggested they go ahead and make dessert for the next day before playing some video games. Grandma then showed Maddie how to read through the recipe and lay out everything they would need for the **Black Forest Gooey Goodness**.

After donning their matching aprons and washing their hands, they talked and giggled while tearing up the angel food cake. They danced to music while spooning the pie filling and making the pudding. When they finished the **Black Forest Gooey Goodness**, they put it in the fridge. Grandma and Maddie continued to dance around the kitchen while they cleaned up their mess. Then they raced to the family room for more video games.

The next day was wonderfully lazy as the whole family watched parades and football. Maddie loved cuddling on the couch with everyone. A little before noon, Grandma nodded to Maddie, and they headed to the kitchen to start lunch. They wiped the dust from the cans of chicken, corn, chiles, and peas, so that the can opener wouldn't push dirt into the food. Grandma did most of the work, so she could show Maddie how to perform each step.

While they were making the **Cornbread Casserole**, Grandma explained to Maddie that many people believe eating black-eyed peas, pork, and cornbread on New Year's Day will bring good luck all year long.

Grandma and Maddie popped the casserole into the oven and prepared the black-eyed peas on the stove top. Maddie set the table. She couldn't wait to show off her new cooking skills to Mom and Dad. When everything was ready, Maddie called Mom and Dad to the table. Everyone sat down, Dad said grace, and they dug into their traditional New Year's Day meal. Over and over, Mom and Dad talked about how good everything tasted.

Maddie was beaming. Her first real meal was a huge success – and a delicious start to a year of holiday cooking.

Easy Cornbread Casserole

2 – 8.5 ounce boxes Jiffy Corn Muffin mix
1 – 4.5 ounce can chopped green chiles, do not drain
1 – 1.25 ounce envelope mild taco seasoning mix
1 – 12 ounce package frozen broccoli and cheese sauce
1 – 12.5 ounce can chunk chicken, do not drain
1 – 8 ounce bag shredded cheddar cheese
1 – 14.75 ounce can cream style corn
4 – taco shells, crumbled

Preheat the oven to 325. Grease a 13x9x2 pan.

In a large mixing bowl, combine the corn muffin mix and taco seasoning.

Stir in the chicken, corn, and chiles and allow the mixture to rest for 2-3 minutes.

Stir the frozen broccoli into the corn muffin mixture and pour the batter into the prepared pan.

Bake the cornbread casserole for 50 minutes.

Sprinkle the cheese and taco shells evenly over the casserole and bake it another 5 minutes.

Good Luck Black-eyed Peas

2 – 15.5 ounce cans black-eyed peas
1 – 2.5 ounce package low sodium real bacon bits
1 – tablespoon dried onion flakes

Dump all the ingredients into a medium saucepan and stir a little.

Heat the black-eyed peas on medium until hot or the juice starts to boil.

Reduce the heat to low until the entire meal is ready to serve.

Black Forest Gooey Goodness

1 – 11 ounce premade angel food cake
1 – 3.5 ounce box instant chocolate pudding mix
1 – 21 ounce can cherry pie filling
1 – 8 ounce tub sour cream
1 – tub whipped cream

Tear the angel food cake into small chunks and spread evenly across the bottom of a 13x9x2 pan.

Spoon the pie filling over the chunks of angel food cake.

In a large mixing bowl, prepare the pudding according to package directions.

When the pudding thickens, switch to a spoon and stir in the sour cream.

Pour the pudding over the cherries and cake and refrigerate for at least 2 hours.

Top with whipped cream just before serving.

Drizzle with chocolate and top with a cherry. (optional)

Notes

Valentine's Day

Grandma was waiting in the parking lot as school let out. Maddie jumped into the car, happy to have a ride home. "It's Valentine's Day," Grandma told Maddie, "and we're going to make a romantic dinner for your parents to share!"

Grandma had already been to the grocery store. As soon as Maddie put away her things, they pulled out the cookbook and laid out all the ingredients for dinner. Maddie watched Grandma's careful measurements and tried to mimic them as they made the batter for the **Chocolate Chip Bundt Cake**. Grandma poured the batter into the Bundt pan and slid the cake into the preheated oven.

"Maddie, you set the timer for the shortest cooking time in the cake recipe," Grandma said. She explained how to test the cake for doneness by inserting a toothpick, to see if the toothpick comes out with batter stuck to it. "Wet batter means the cake is not done, and we need to set the timer for 5 or 10 more minutes, until the toothpick comes out clean or with only a couple cake crumbs."

While the cake was baking, Grandma let Maddie make the **Dreamy Horseradish Salad Dressing** all by herself. Maddie had to stand on a stool to be tall enough to beat the cream. Under Grandma's watchful eye, she made beautiful, thick soft peaks of cream and added the remaining ingredients. As they put the salad dressing in the fridge, the timer went off – time for the first toothpick test! The cake was already done, so they put it on a rack to cool.

In the meantime, Grandma instructed Maddie to set the table for two and put candles in the center of the table for her parents to light (Grandma and Maddie would eat in the kitchen). With the table set, Grandma and Maddie could relax. At 6 p.m., they would make the **Creamy Beef Stroganoff.**

Grandma showed Maddie how to crumble the ground beef while it browned. They opened all the jars and packages so the ingredients would be ready when the hamburger was brown. They added each ingredient as the recipe stated. Then, while the stroganoff simmered on the stove, they inverted the cake and cut generous slices for dessert.

The dining table looked beautiful – just perfect for a romantic dinner for two. Maddie had used the good china and silver to set the table. She then filled the water glasses and put a small flower arrangement in the middle of the table. Next, she filled the salad bowls with lettuce and placed them just-so. Salt, pepper, salad dressing, matches: everything was there.

When the stroganoff was done, Maddie ushered Mom and Dad into the dining room. Mom and Dad were delighted! Maddie helped them light the candles as Grandma brought in the bowl of stroganoff and scrumptious slices of cake. Maddie turned off the lights as she and Grandma headed to the kitchen. Grandma winked at Maddie as they started to eat. Maddie knew her parents would enjoy the wonderful dinner she and Grandma had prepared.

"Thanks, Grandma," she said as they ate, "I didn't know making nice dinners could be so much fun!"

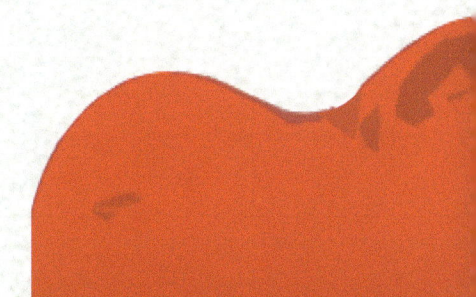

Creamy Beef Stroganoff

1 – pound lean ground beef
2¼ – cups buttermilk
1 – 6 ounce jar sliced mushrooms, do not drain
2 – tablespoons sugar
1 – 5.5 ounce box Hamburger Helper Deluxe Beef Stroganoff

In a 10–inch skillet, brown and crumble the ground beef over medium high heat; do not drain.

Add the mushrooms and bring the meat to a boil.

Stir in the Hamburger Helper seasoning packet, buttermilk, sugar, and Hamburger Helper noodles, in that order.

When the sauce returns to a boil, reduce the heat to low and simmer the stroganoff for about 10 more minutes, stirring occasionally.

As soon as the noodles are soft and the sauce is thick, serve the stroganoff.

Dreamy Horseradish Salad

1 – cup heavy whipping cream
¼ – teaspoon paprika
1 – teaspoon salt
3 – tablespoons grated horseradish
1 – teaspoon sugar
3 – tablespoons spiced vinegar or lemon juice
½ – teaspoon ground mustard
1 - 12 ounce bag shredded lettuce

In a large mixing bowl with a mixer on high speed, beat the cream until soft peaks form.

Reduce the speed to medium and blend in the remaining ingredients except the lettuce.

Pour the dressing into a cruet and chill for a few hours.

At serving time, shake the cruet and pour the dressing over the lettuce.

Chocolate Chip Bundt Cake

1 – 13x9x2 box chocolate fudge cake mix
1¾ – cups half-n-half or milk
1 – 3.9 ounce box instant chocolate pudding mix
1 – 12 ounce bag semisweet chocolate chips
2 – eggs
Cool Whip and fresh raspberries

Preheat the oven to 350.

Grease and flour a 10–inch tube pan.

In a large mixing bowl, combine the cake mix and pudding mix.

Beat in the eggs and half-n-half with a mixer on low speed.

Stir in the chocolate chips by hand.

Pour the batter into the tube pan and bake the cake for 50–60 minutes, until a toothpick comes out clean.

Cool the cake to room temperature before removing it from the pan.

Serve each slice of cake with a dollop of Cool Whip and a sprinkling of raspberries.

Notes

Happy Easter

Maddie got up early to get ready for church. Grandma called and reminded her to take the hash browns out of the freezer, so they could thaw. Maddie and her parents would pick up Grandma on the way to church and sit in their favorite pew with their friends, singing and praying. Maddie was excited about the special festivities on Easter Sunday.

After church, Grandma came home with Maddie and her parents. Grandma and Maddie put on their matching aprons and took over the kitchen. Mom had already picked up a spiral sliced ham on Saturday, so the duo had only a few dishes to make.

Grandma let Maddie read the recipes out loud. As usual, they arranged all the ingredients neatly on the counter.

"The **Dijon Vinaigrette** needs time to chill, so let's make that first," Grandma suggested. Maddie measured each ingredient and poured it into the cruet, as Grandma watched. Maddie shook the cruet and placed it in the fridge.

Next, Grandma and Maddie made the **Aaaaw Gratin Potatoes**. Grandma let Maddie do most of the work now, as Maddie was getting very good at following the recipes and measuring the ingredients. Maddie updated Grandma on all the latest school events while they worked. Grandma helped Maddie pour the cheese sauce over the potatoes, and they popped the potatoes into the oven.

After that, Maddie poured each ingredient of the **Crusty Cobbler** across the pan, trying to keep each layer even. Grandma helped Maddie slide the cobbler into the oven next to the potatoes. They took off their aprons and headed to the family room. They knew it would be okay for the cobbler to finish shortly after the potatoes, so the cobbler could cool a bit while they were eating.

When the timer rang for the potatoes, Maddie set the table while Grandma carried all the food to the dining room. Maddie filled the salad bowls and brought in the salad dressing she had made. Later, they would bring out the cobbler and vanilla ice cream.

Maddie was feeling so proud of her expanding skills as a cook. So were her parents! In fact, her mom, sitting down at the table, commented, "I think I'm beginning to enjoy Maddie's Christmas gift almost as much as Maddie!"

Dijon Vinaigrette Salad

¾ – cup red wine vinegar
1 – teaspoon lemon pepper
¼ – cup olive oil
1 – teaspoon garlic salt
1 – generous tablespoon Dijon mustard
1 – teaspoon dill weed
1 - 12 ounce bag shredded lettuce

Combine all the ingredients, except the lettuce, in a small cruet and refrigerate.

At serving time, shake the cruet and pour the dressing over the lettuce.

Aaaaw Gratin Potatoes

½ – cup margarine
1 – small onion, chopped
1 – 8 ounce block sharp cheddar cheese, cut in chunks
1 – 16 ounce bar Velveeta cheese, cut in chunks
1 – 2 pound bag frozen Southern style hash browns, thawed
1 – pint half-n-half

Preheat the oven to 350. In a large saucepan over medium heat, combine the margarine, onion, cheeses, and half-n-half.

Salt and pepper to taste. Stir the sauce occasionally until the chunks of cheese are mostly melted.

Spread the hash browns evenly across the bottom of a 13x9x2 Pyrex baking dish.

Pour the cheese sauce over the hash browns.

Bake the potatoes 60–90 minutes, until brown and bubbly on top.

Crusty Cobbler

2 – 13x9x2 boxes white cake mix
1 – 12 ounce can 7UP
1 – 40 ounce bag frozen mixed berries

Preheat the oven to 350.

Generously grease a 13x9x3 lasagna pan.

Spread one of the dry cake mixes evenly across the bottom of the pan.

Arrange the frozen fruit in an even layer over the cake mix.

Sprinkle the remaining dry cake mix over the fruit, filling in the cracks a little.

Drizzle the 7UP over the cake mix; do not stir.

Bake the cobbler for 45–50 minutes, until the topping becomes light brown and crusty.

Remove the cobbler from the oven and let it sit for 5 minutes before serving.

Notes

Mother's Day
Breakfast in Bed

Maddie's alarm went off. She knew she would have to get up early to surprise Mom and Grandma with breakfasts in bed.

Dad met Maddie in the kitchen to help her get everything in the oven and prepare two trays to carry breakfast to Mom and Grandma.

Grandma and Maddie had already prepared the **Ham n' Cheese Breakfast Casserole,** Jell-O for **Black Cherry Salad**, and **Caramel Monkey Bread** the night before. It had been difficult for Maddie to keep her secret, but she really wanted to surprise Grandma with breakfast in bed instead of having Grandma help her serve Mom. It was a wonderful way to show them both how much she appreciated everything they did for her.

While breakfast was cooking, Maddie showed Dad how to read the recipe to finish the **Black Cherry Salad.** She missed Grandma's help in the kitchen, but she also liked sharing the experience with her father. She laid out the ingredients, and Dad helped her prepare the half-n-half and marshmallows. Together, they stirred in the final ingredients and spread the topping over the Jell-O. The salad could chill while the casserole finished cooking.

Maddie pulled the clean dishes from the dishwasher and put them away. She wanted to do the dishes quickly after breakfast, so Mom and Grandma would see a beautiful, clean kitchen after they showered and dressed.

The trays looked beautiful as Dad and Maddie filled the plates, poured the juice and coffee, and added a bud vase with a single rose. Dad carried the trays as Maddie burst into each bedroom to deliver joyful morning hugs and the best breakfast she had ever made.

Mom and Grandma had what every mom wants on Mother's Day: time with the people they love. Maddie felt a warm glow inside that she had never felt before, as she became more and more aware of the ways in which lovingly prepared food can bring families together.

Ham n' Cheese Breakfast Casserole

- 10 – slices bread, cubed
- 2 – cups milk
- 2 – pounds ham, cubed
- 1 – teaspoon salt
- 1 – 16 ounce bag shredded cheddar cheese, divided
- 2 – teaspoons ground mustard
- 8 – eggs
- ½ – teaspoon garlic powder

Generously butter a 13x9x2 pan and spread half of the bread across the bottom of the pan.

Sprinkle the meat and most of the cheese over the bread and top with the remaining bread.

In a large mixing bowl, whisk the eggs until foamy. Beat in the milk, salt, mustard, and garlic powder and pour the egg mixture over the top layer of bread.

Pack down the casserole using a potato masher until all the bread is moist and refrigerate the casserole overnight.

Preheat the oven to 350. Bake the casserole for 40–60 minutes.

Top the casserole with the rest of the cheese during the last 10 minutes of baking.

Black Cherry Salad

Salad:
2 – 15 ounce cans pitted dark sweet cherries
1 – 3 ounce box dark cherry Jell-O
1 – 15.25 ounce can crushed pineapple

Topping:
½ – cup half-n-half or milk
½ – cup chopped pecans, optional
20 – regular size marshmallows
1 – 8 ounce tub Cool Whip, thawed

Drain the cherries and pineapple to make 1¾ cups of juice. Put the juice in a small saucepan over medium high heat. Bring the juice almost to a boil and dissolve the Jell-O in the juice. Meanwhile, spread the cherries across the bottom of a 2.2-quart shallow dish. When the Jell-O is dissolved, pour it over the cherries and refrigerate until set.

In a large saucepan over low heat, warm the half-n-half and marshmallows until the marshmallows have melted, stirring regularly. Remove the pan from the heat and stir in the pecans and crushed pineapple. Fold in the Cool Whip and spread the topping over the Jell-O. Refrigerate the salad until serving time. Top with berries.

Caramel Monkey Bread

1 – bag of 12 frozen yeast rolls
½ – cup brown sugar
1 – cup chopped pecans
½ – teaspoon cinnamon
1 – 3.4 ounce box butterscotch pudding mix
½ – cup butter, melted

Grease a tube pan, including the cone. Place the frozen rolls evenly around the bottom of the pan.

Sprinkle the pecans, pudding mix, brown sugar, and cinnamon evenly over the rolls, one at a time in that order. Drizzle the butter over all. Cover the tube pan with plastic wrap and leave the rolls on the counter overnight to rise.

Preheat the oven to 350. Remove the plastic wrap and bake the monkey bread for 25 minutes, until the bread is brown and cooked in the middle.

Invert the pan onto a serving tray as soon as you take the bread out of the oven.

Notes

Father's Day

Saturday morning, Maddie pulled out the **Banana Pudding Cake** recipe and read it out loud. She turned on the oven and lined up the ingredients while Grandma watched. Maddie made the cake batter – and Grandma helped her pour it into the prepared pan. While the cake baked, Grandma and Maddie made the **Coleslaw** and put it in the fridge. When the cake was finished baking, they pulled it from the oven to cool.

While they worked, Grandma told stories about Maddie's Mom and Dad when they were dating, like the first time Dad tried to cook dinner and charred the chicken so bad it stuck to the grill! Maddie loved to hear family stories and asked Grandma to tell her more.

Dad loved sports, and Maddie wanted to make sure Dad would have plenty of time to sprawl out in his favorite chair and watch every game on TV. Maddie ran outside to cut the grass for Dad. She even put the trash in the barrel out back. Sports all afternoon and Dad's favorite dinner would make a perfect Father's Day.

Sunday morning, Mom helped Maddie cut up the onion. Maddie showed Mom how she could read the recipe and prepare the roast all by herself. Mom smiled as she watched Maddie put all the ingredients into the crockpot and turn it on low. Then, they got ready for church.

Grandma came home with them after church and helped Maddie prepare the topping for the cake. Maddie pulled out her favorite stool, so she could use the mixer while Grandma sliced the bananas. Layer by layer, they finished the **Banana Pudding Cake**, and if they nibbled on a few vanilla wafers along the way, no one would know but them!

Later that afternoon, as they cleaned up and put the dirty dishes in the dishwasher, it got quiet for a minute. Maddie was thinking about how good she was at reading the recipes and preparing the kitchen. She had remembered to buy Dad's favorite barbeque sauce for the pork roast and extra half-n-half for the cake, ensuring Dad's thumbs-up on the perfect meal. Grandma was thinking about how much she treasured the time she spent helping Maddie learn to cook. She hadn't realized it at the time, but that little cookbook had been as much a gift to herself as to Maddie.

Pulled Pork

1 – medium onion
¼ – teaspoon cayenne pepper
1 – 3 pound pork shoulder or butt
¼ – cup apple cider vinegar
1 – tablespoon freeze-dried minced garlic
3 – tablespoons Worcestershire sauce
1½ – teaspoons ground mustard
2 – 12 ounce cans Dr Pepper

Cut the onion into eighths and spread the pieces on the bottom of a crockpot.

Lay the pork roast on top of the onion.

In a small bowl, combine the garlic, mustard, cayenne, vinegar, and Worcestershire and pour over the roast.

Pour the Dr Pepper over the pork roast. Cook the roast on low for at least 8 hours.

When the roast is done, shred the entire roast using 2 forks. Put the shredded pork back into the crockpot with all that juice and cook it another hour.

Use a slotted spoon to remove the shredded pork from the crockpot and discard the juices. Serve the pulled pork with your favorite barbeque sauce with sides or as a sandwich.

Potatoes Parmesan

½ – cup butter
2 – tablespoons flour
2½ – pounds small new potatoes, do not peel
½ – cup grated parmesan cheese

Preheat the oven to 350. Put the butter in a 13x9x2 pan and place the pan in the oven just until the butter melts. Clean the potatoes and cut them into chunks.

Combine the flour and parmesan cheese in a plastic bag. Drop the wet chunks of potato into the cheese and shake. Place the coated potatoes in the melted butter.

Salt and pepper to taste. Bake the potatoes for 30 minutes and use tongs to turn over all the potatoes. Bake the potatoes another 30 minutes.

Cole Slaw

1 – 16 ounce bag shredded cabbage for slaw
1 – 12 ounce jar Marie's Coleslaw Dressing

Dump the shredded cabbage into a large bowl.

Pour the jar of dressing over the cabbage and stir.

Cover the coleslaw and store it in the refrigerator.

Banana Pudding Cake

Cake:
1 – 13x9x2 box yellow cake mix
1/3 – cup sugar
3 – large ripe bananas

Topping:
2 – 3.4 ounce boxes instant banana cream pudding mix
1 – 8 ounce tub Cool Whip, thawed
3 – large barely-ripe bananas, sliced
1 – 11 ounce box vanilla wafers

Preheat the oven to 350. Grease the bottom of a lasagna pan, 13x9x3. Prepare the cake mix according to the package directions, substituting half-n-half for the water. Mash the ripe bananas and stir them with the sugar. Blend the mashed bananas into the cake batter and pour the batter into the prepared pan. Bake the cake according to package directions, until a toothpick comes out clean. Cool the cake to room temperature.

In a large mixing bowl, prepare the pudding mix according to package directions, using half-n-half or whipping cream instead of milk. When the pudding is thick, stir in the sliced bananas and layer the pudding over the cake. Carefully, spread the Cool Whip over the pudding and cover the entire top with side-by-side vanilla wafers. Refrigerate the cake for several hours before serving.

Notes

Fourth of July Picnic

Fireworks rule! Grandma and Maddie discussed the National Anthem and how fireworks represented the "rockets' red glare" that Francis Scott Key, author of "The Star-Spangled Banner," saw as our country fought for independence. Maddie enjoyed reviewing history while they cooked and also showing Grandma all the interesting things that she learned in school. Giggling, Maddie asked Grandma if she knew Mr. Key when she was younger. They both laughed.

It was Maddie's turn to bring dessert to the family Fourth of July picnic. This would be the first time Maddie would bring a dish that she made with her own two hands, and she couldn't wait to show her cousins what a good cook she was becoming. She and Grandma decided to make a flag cake that would look as beautiful as it tasted.

The cake would be cut after dinner, so Maddie talked Grandma into letting her make two batches of **Finger Jell-O**. Grandma was thrilled that Maddie was so eager to spend more time in the kitchen, so she happily approved anything Maddie wanted to prepare. The cookbook was inspiring a new chef in the family!

Maddie prepared the cake batter while Grandma mashed the strawberries and poured them into the batter. Grandma then helped Maddie pour the batter into the pan and they slid the cake into the oven. Next, they started two pans of **finger Jell-O**. One pan would be strawberry red, and the other pan berry blue. Very patriotic!

As they stirred all the gelatin into the boiling water, Grandma and Maddie talked about the science behind **finger Jell-O**, how the cream would rise to the top as the Jell-O gelled in the fridge. When the gelatin was dissolved, Maddie made blue and Grandma made red, they stirred in the cream and poured each of the Jell-Os into shallow pans and popped them into the fridge. When the cake was done, they set it out to cool, put the cream cheese in a mixing bowl to soften, rinsed off the remaining berries, and headed to the family room for video games.

About an hour before they had to leave for the picnic, Grandma watched Maddie climb up on the stool and beat the cream cheese, Cool Whip, and powdered sugar. They spread the topping over the cake and added the berries to make a flag – it looked perfect!

As they cut the **finger Jell-O** into bitesize cubes and alternated the colors on a serving tray, Maddie told Grandma about Betsy Ross and the different versions of the flag they had discussed in school.

Maddie was excited about the picnic and fireworks. She knew that she would have fun playing in the park with her cousins and that they would enjoy her treats as they got tired and hungry. When it got dark, everyone would sit on blankets and watch the best fireworks in the whole world.

Independence Day Strawberry Cake

Cake:
1 – 13x9x2 box white cake mix
1 – cup vegetable oil
1 – 3 ounce box strawberry Jell-O
¼ – cup half-n-half
4 – eggs
1 – pound fresh strawberries, mashed

Frosting:
1 – 8 ounce bar cream cheese, softened
1 – pound fresh strawberries
1 – 8 ounce tub Cool Whip, thawed
1 – pint fresh blueberries
½ – cup powdered sugar

Preheat the oven to 350. Grease a 13x9x2 pan. In a large mixing bowl, combine the cake mix and dry Jell-O. With a mixer on medium speed, beat in the eggs, oil, and half-n-half until well blended. Manually stir in the mashed strawberries. Pour the cake batter into the prepared pan and bake the cake for 25–35 minutes, until a toothpick comes out clean. Cool the cake to room temperature.

In a large mixing bowl with a mixer on medium speed, beat the cream cheese, Cool Whip, and powdered sugar until well blended. Spread the frosting over the cake and decorate like an American Flag. Use the blueberries to make a square in the upper left hand corner. Slice the strawberries to make stripes across the cake. Store the cake in the fridge.

Berries n' Cream Finger Jell-O

4 – cups water
4 – .25 ounce envelopes unflavored gelatin
2 – 6 ounce boxes strawberry or berry blue Jell-O
1 – cup heavy whipping cream, do not whip

In a medium saucepan over high heat, bring the water to a boil.

Remove the pan from the heat and pour in the Jell-O and gelatin, stirring until the gelatin is completely dissolved.

Stir in the cream and pour the Jell-O into a shallow 2.2-quart Pyrex dish.

Refrigerate the Jell-O until set.

Notes

41

Halloween

Maddie loved trick-or-treating. Everyone in her neighborhood decorated their house; some were very scary. Mom always helped Maddie make the best costumes, in hopes the neighbors would not be able to recognize her as she hurried door-to-door to fill her bag. Maddie tingled as she approached each house. She tried to look her scariest as each neighbor opened the door and offered sweets to keep the ghouls from entering.

Maddie came home with a full bag of every candy imaginable. While Mom greeted the last few trick-or-treaters, Grandma and Maddie sorted through her candy. She picked out her favorites and set aside the rest to make treats for the next day: All Saints' Day.

Their church always had an All Saints' Day party the day after Halloween, and Maddie enjoyed taking homemade treats to share with everyone.

Maddie counted out twenty-four Reese's peanut butter cups to set aside for the **Peanut Butter Tarts**. Grandma explained that they should make the **Pretzel Bites** first, since they required a low oven temperature. They had plenty of miniature candy bars, and Grandma started unwrapping the candies while Maddie pulled out the biggest jellyroll pan they had.

Maddie carefully laid out the pretzels nose-to-nose on the pan and Grandma placed a candy bar on each pretzel. After Grandma unwrapped the last candy bar, they checked the thermostat in the oven. It was the correct temperature, so they popped the **Pretzel Bites** into the oven. Grandma explained to Maddie how important it was to have a thermometer in the oven to make sure the oven thermostat was working properly. If the oven temperature didn't match the recipe, their treats could burn or not cook in the middle.

Next, Grandma pulled out the mini-muffin tin, and they started preparing the **Peanut Butter Tarts**. When the **Pretzel Bites** were done, they pulled the treats out of the oven and raised the oven temperature. Grandma and Maddie covered the **Pretzel Bites** with a long sheet of waxed paper and laughed while they smashed each candy bar with their thumbs. Ooooey Gooey! Once the tarts were baking, Maddie started on the brownies. As soon as the tarts were done, she slid the brownies into the oven.

It was getting close to bedtime, so Maddie went to her room to get ready for bed. She put on her pajamas and brushed her teeth. Then she went back out to the kitchen to help Grandma clean up. They put the dishes in the dishwasher and wiped down the counters. When the brownies were done, they put the pan on a rack and turned off the oven.

Maddie was so tired she fell into bed. What a wonderful day! Full of costumes, candy, and an evening spent in the kitchen with Grandma – one of the nicest treats of the day.

Pretzel Bites

½ – 6 ounce bag miniature heart–shaped pretzels
Any miniature candy bars

Preheat the oven to 200.

Line a large cookie sheet with wax paper.

Lay the pretzels flat on the wax paper, one pretzel for each candy bar.

Unwrap the candy and set one candy bar in the center of each pretzel.

Bake the pretzels for 10 minutes.

As soon as you remove the pretzels from the oven, lay a sheet of wax paper over the candy.

Squish each candy bar into its pretzel by pressing on the wax paper with your thumb.

Refrigerate the treats for 2 hours and the wax paper will peel right off.

Serve at room temperature.

Peanut Butter Tarts

1 – cup sugar
1 – egg
1 – cup peanut butter
24 – ROLO caramels or Reese's mini-peanut butter cups

Preheat the oven to 350. Line a 24–mini–muffin tin with foil cupcake liners.

In a small mixing bowl, stir together the sugar, peanut butter, and egg until well blended.

Using a melon–baller, make 24 balls of dough and drop each one into a muffin cup.

Press a piece of candy, wide–end up, into each ball of peanut butter, about half way into the dough.

Bake the tarts for 12–20 minutes, until the chocolate is melting and the cookies are turning brown around the edges.

Cool the tarts on a wire rack.

Candy Bar Brownies

1 – 13x9x2 box of your favorite fudge brownie mix
Any miniature candy bars - about 1 pound

Prepare the brownie mix according to the instructions on the box.

Cut the candy bars into small chunks and stir them with the brownie batter.

Spread the batter evenly across the bottom of a 13x9x2 pan and bake the brownies according to the package directions.

Cool the brownies for 10 minutes and run a knife all the way around the edge of the brownies to separate them from the pan.

Allow the brownies to cool to room temperature before cutting.

Notes

Grandma came over Wednesday afternoon to begin her holiday cooking ritual with Maddie, who read the recipes while Grandma helped lay out ingredients and make a list of items still needed. After a quick trip to the grocery store, they were ready to prepare the feast.

Though she had grown over the year, Maddie still needed to climb onto her stool to beat the eggs for the **Pumpkin Pie Cake** and prepare the batter. Grandma helped Maddie pour the batter into the pan and slide the cake into the oven. While the cake was baking, they wrapped the green beans in bacon strips, covered the pan with plastic wrap, and put the **Haystacks** in the fridge. When the cake was done, they put it on a rack to cool.

Maddie pulled out the potato masher and began mashing the cranberries. Grandma put two packages of Cool Whip in the fridge to thaw. They added the sugar and marshmallows to the cranberries, covered the bowl, and left it on the counter for the next day. Grandma explained to Maddie that the sugar would draw the juice out of the mashed berries and sweeten and soften the cranberries for the salad. They headed for the family room for video games.

After breakfast the next morning, Grandma cut up the apples and grapes for the **Cranberry Fluff** fruit salad while Maddie stirred everything together. They covered the bowl and placed it in the fridge. Next, they frosted the cake with a tub of Cool Whip and put the cake back in the fridge. Grandma and Maddie practiced their royal wave as they performed their best gliding walk to the family room to watch the parades. They loved to wave at the floats on TV and choose their favorite balloon characters.

About 90 minutes before they wanted to eat, Maddie grabbed Grandma's hand and led her to the kitchen. Grandma took a minute to explain the importance of all the dishes being ready at the same time. So first they put the butter in a pan to melt for the green beans and started making the stuffing. Grandma explained they would have to cook the **Haystacks** a little longer than the recipe listed because the pan of green beans had been in the fridge all night and the recipe cooking time was based on room temperature. That meant the sweet potatoes and the green beans would be in the oven the same amount of time. Perfect!

Grandma and Maddie put the sweet potatoes, brown sugar, and apricots in a pan and set it aside to put in the oven with the green beans. Next, they put the turkey on the stove to brown. By then, the butter was melted, and Maddie stirred in the brown sugar, garlic, and soy sauce. Grandma poured the sauce over the green beans, and they slipped the sweet potatoes and green beans into the oven.

As they worked, Grandma explained to Maddie that Thanksgiving was one of her favorite holidays. Not only did Thanksgiving stand for family and gratitude, it was truly an American tradition.

When the timer rang, Grandma started carrying the food to the table while Maddie called Mom and Dad to dinner. Everyone sat down and bowed their heads. As Dad said grace, Maddie felt a warm sense of gratitude fill her heart. She was truly thankful for such a wonderful family and the love she felt every day. Grandma was thankful to see how Maddie was embracing her new role as family chef, all thanks to that little cookbook.

Turkey and Stuffing

2 – tablespoons butter
1 – 6 ounce box turkey flavored stuffing mix
1½ – pounds turkey steaks
½ – cup milk or cream
1 – 10.75 ounce can condensed cream of chicken soup
1 – 8 ounce package shredded cheddar cheese

Make the stuffing according to the package directions.

Meanwhile, melt the butter in a large skillet over medium high heat.

Brown the turkey on both sides and reduce the heat to low.

Fluff the stuffing and spoon it on top of the turkey.

Lift the turkey steaks to make sure they aren't stuck to the bottom of the pan.

In a small mixing bowl, blend the soup and milk and pour the soup over the turkey and stuffing.

Cover the pan and simmer 5 minutes.

Sprinkle the cheese over the stuffing, replace the lid, and simmer another 5-10 minutes, until the turkey is cooked through.

Remove the pan from the heat and wait 5 minutes before serving.

Cranberry Fluff

- 2 – cups cranberries
- 1 – cup halved red seedless grapes
- ¾ – cup sugar
- ½ – cup chopped pecans
- 3 – cups miniature marshmallows
- ½ – teaspoon salt
- 2 – Braeburn apples, peeled and chopped
- 1 – 8 ounce tub Cool Whip, thawed

Mash the cranberries in a flat–bottomed 3-quart dish.

Sprinkle the sugar over the cranberries and stir in the marshmallows.

Leave the cranberries on the counter overnight.

In the morning, stir in the apples, grapes, pecans, salt, and Cool Whip, in that order.

Refrigerate the fluff until serving time.

Sweet Potato Casserole

1 – 40 ounce can sweet potatoes
1 – cup brown sugar
1 – 10 ounce jar apricot Simply Fruit
¼ – cup chopped walnuts

Preheat the oven to 350.

Generously grease a 9x9x2 pan.

Drain the sweet potatoes, reserving ¼ cup syrup.

Spread the sweet potatoes across the bottom of the pan and drizzle the ¼ cup syrup over the potatoes.

Sprinkle the brown sugar over the sweet potatoes.

Stir the fruit to loosen it up and spoon the apricots over the sweet potatoes and brown sugar.

Bake the casserole for 45 minutes, until bubbly in the center.

Sprinkle the walnuts over the casserole during the last 5 minutes of baking.

Haystacks

2 – pounds fresh green beans
½ – cup brown sugar
1 – pound bacon
1 – teaspoon garlic salt
½ – cup butter
1 – tablespoon soy sauce

Preheat the oven to 350. Use a pan just big enough to hold all the haystacks in one layer. Break off the stem on the end of each bean and discard the stems.
If the beans are extra-long, cut them in half.

Wrap 6–8 beans in a half strip of bacon and push a toothpick through the bacon to hold it in place. Lay each haystack in the pan.

Melt the butter in a small saucepan over low heat. Remove the butter from the heat and stir in the brown sugar, garlic salt, and soy sauce. Pour the syrup over the haystacks. Bake the green beans for 30–45 minutes, until the bacon is done and the syrup is thick and bubbly.

Pumpkin Pie Cake

1 – 30 ounce can pumpkin pie mix
1 – 13x9x2 box butter pecan cake mix
½ – cup applesauce
1 – 8 ounce tub Cool Whip, thawed
3 – eggs

Preheat the oven to 350.

Grease and flour a 13x9x2 pan.

In a large bowl with a mixer on medium, beat the pumpkin, applesauce, and eggs.

Reduce the speed to low and add the cake mix, beating until well blended.

Pour the batter into the prepared pan and bake for 35–45 minutes, until a toothpick comes out clean.

Cool the cake and frost it with the Cool Whip.

Refrigerate the cake until serving time.

Notes

Grandma danced into the kitchen on Christmas Eve, singing carols. Maddie was already there, ready to go, listening to her parents singing along from the living room.

Maddie had learned so much about cooking over the last year. She knew to read the recipes thoroughly before beginning. She had already laid out all the ingredients for the **Seven Layer Salad** and **Mini-Cheesecakes**, and the cream cheese was in the mixing bowl to soften.

Maddie looked so cute in her apron as she washed her hands and wiped off the counter. Grandma was so proud as she pulled out her apron to help Maddie. They were truly a chef team now, standing side-by-side as they prepared each dish. Grandma still did most of the knife work, as Maddie layered the salad together.

Once the salad was covered and placed in the fridge, they started on the cheesecakes. Grandma stood back and watched Maddie expertly beat the cheesecake batter. Grandma exclaimed, "My, what a wonderful cook you have become!"

Maddie glowed as the two of them poured the cheesecake batter into the cupcake pan. They popped the cheesecakes into the oven and a couple of vanilla wafers into their mouths, winking and smiling at each other.

Maddie was excited about tomorrow; opening presents, playing with all her new toys, and preparing dinner. She thought about last Christmas, and how unsure she had felt when she opened the cookbook-and-aprons gift from Grandma. Now, she knew it was one of her favorite gifts EVER. Not only did she learn to cook, but she and Grandma had shared so much time, love, and fun together – with more still to come! Maddie wasn't sure if Grandma could come up with a better gift for tomorrow, but she was excited to find out!

Lasagna

1 – 7 ounce tub ricotta cheese
½ – teaspoon basil
2 – eggs
1 – teaspoon freeze-dried chives
½ – teaspoon garlic powder
1 – 9 ounce box ready-to-use lasagna noodles
½ – teaspoon oregano
1 – 16 ounce bag shredded mozzarella cheese
2 – 45 ounce jars prepared spaghetti sauce

Preheat the oven to 350. In a medium mixing bowl, combine the ricotta cheese, eggs, garlic powder, oregano, basil, and chives.

In a 13x9x3 lasagna pan, lay out 3 or 4 lasagna noodles, whatever you need to cover the bottom of the pan. Pour 1 jar of spaghetti sauce evenly over the noodles.

Cover the sauce layer with another layer of noodles. Spread the ricotta cheese mixture evenly over the noodles. Sprinkle 1 cup of mozzarella cheese over the ricotta. Cover the cheese with another layer of noodles. Pour the other jar of spaghetti sauce over the noodles. Top the lasagna with lots and lots of mozzarella cheese.

Loosely cover the lasagna with foil, shiny side down, and bake for about 30 minutes. Remove the foil covering and bake a few more minutes, until bubbly and brown on top. Let the lasagna cool for 10 minutes before serving.

Garlic Sticks

¾ – cup butter
2 – teaspoons garlic salt
3 – 11 ounce tubes of refrigerated breadsticks

Preheat the oven to 350. In a small pan over low heat, melt the butter and stir in the garlic salt. Keep the butter warm.

Choose a small jellyroll pan that will barely hold the bread and line the pan with foil, shiny side down. Twist 2 breadsticks together and stretch them lengthwise.

Arrange the sticks of dough in a single layer across the pan, close together or touching. Drizzle a little garlic butter over each breadstick, using a little less than half of the butter.

Bake the breadsticks for 20–25 minutes, until medium brown on top. Pull the ends of the foil away from the pan so the foil touches the breadsticks and forms a cup all the way around.

Drizzle the rest of the garlic butter over the hot breadsticks and allow the butter to soak in.

Mini-Cheesecakes

12 – vanilla wafers
2 – eggs
2 – 8 ounce bars cream cheese, softened
1 – teaspoon vanilla
½ – cup sugar
1 - jar strawberry preserves

Preheat the oven to 325. Line a 12–cup regular-size muffin tin with foil liners. Place a vanilla wafer on the bottom of each liner.

In a large mixing bowl with a mixer on medium speed, beat the cream cheese, sugar, eggs, and vanilla until well blended. Pour the cream cheese mixture over each vanilla wafer until each cup is ¾ full.

Bake the mini-cheesecakes for 25–35 minutes, until golden brown on top. Cool the cheesecake cups to room temperature before removing them from the pan.

Refrigerate the mini–cheesecakes until serving time. Top each of the cheesecakes with a spoonful of the preserves.

Seven Layer Salad

- 1 – 12 ounce bag shredded iceberg lettuce
- 1 – 16 ounce bag shredded cheddar jack cheese
- ½ – small chopped onion, optional
- 1 – cup mayonnaise
- 1 – cup chopped celery, optional
- ¼ – cup sugar
- 1 – cup chopped green bell pepper, optional
- 1 – pound bacon, fried and crumbled
- 1 – 10.8 ounce bag frozen peas

In an 11¾x8x3 (17 cup) plastic dish, layer the lettuce, onion, celery, bell pepper, peas, and cheese, in that order.

Carefully spread the mayonnaise over the cheese.

Sprinkle the sugar evenly over the mayonnaise and cover it with the warm bacon.

Refrigerate the salad overnight. Do not toss this salad.

Notes

About the Author:

Valerie Doty was born and raised in the Quad City area, a region of five cities in northwest Illinois and southeastern Iowa, where she acquired an affinity for, and expertise in preparing, Midwestern comfort food from the wonderful cooks in her family.

With a bachelor's degree in Math Theory, she initially joined the world of Information Technology as the industry was skyrocketing in the Dallas, TX area. During her career in that field, Valerie met many coworkers who didn't cook for themselves at all. That lack of kitchen activity inspired her first book and kickstarted Valerie's mission to encourage people to return to the kitchen, bond with family members through cooking, and learn and save all their family favorite recipes.

Valerie spends most of her spare time writing, enjoying her horses, and volunteering.

About the Illustrator:

Katherine Jones was born in the Acadiana area of south Louisiana, where she got her start working in the world of mass media. From there, Kathy spent 20+ years in the world of radio broadcasting before transitioning into graphic design exclusively.

Now, she works as a Custom Lettering Artist, designing logos and artwork for cheerleading teams nationwide. There, as in radio, the essence of her work is to communicate with a creative voice. Kathy is well-traveled and a good writer with finely honed communication skills and an eye for excellent design.

Katherine enjoys cooking for her friends and family, especially during the holidays.

Used With Love but Without Permission: 7UP, Braeburn, Bundt, Cool Whip, Dijon, Dr Pepper, Hamburger Helper, Jell-O, Jiffy, Marie's, Pyrex, Reese's, Rolo, Simply Fruit, Velveeta, and Worcestershire.

www.ingramcontent.com/pod-product-compliance
Lightning Source LLC
Chambersburg PA
CBHW041542220426
43664CB00002B/32